EUROPEAN COUNTRIES TODAY
AUSTRIA

EUROPEAN COUNTRIES TODAY

TITLES IN THE SERIES

Austria	Italy
Belgium	Netherlands
Czech Republic	Poland
Denmark	Portugal
France	Spain
Germany	Sweden
Greece	United Kingdom
Ireland	European Union Facts & Figures

EUROPEAN COUNTRIES TODAY
AUSTRIA

Dominic J. Ainsley

MASON CREST

Mason Crest
450 Parkway Drive, Suite D
Broomall, Pennsylvania PA 19008
(866) MCP-BOOK (toll free)

Copyright © 2019 by Mason Crest, an imprint of National Highlights, Inc. All rights reserved. No part of this publication may be reproduced or transmitted in any form or by any means, electronic or mechanical, including photocopying, recording, taping, or any information storage and retrieval system, without permission in writing from the publisher.

First printing
9 8 7 6 5 4 3 2 1

ISBN: 978-1-4222-3978-0
Series ISBN: 978-1-4222-3977-3
ebook ISBN: 978-1-4222-7793-5

Library of Congress Cataloging-in-Publication Data

Names: Ainsley, Dominic J., author.
Title: Austria / Dominic J. Ainsley.
Description: Broomall, Pennsylvania : Mason Crest, 2019. | Series: European countries today | Includes index.
Identifiers: LCCN 2018007568 (print) | LCCN 2018015417 (ebook) | ISBN 9781422277935 (eBook) | ISBN 9781422239780 (hardback)
Subjects: LCSH: Austria--Juvenile literature.
Classification: LCC DB17 (ebook) | LCC DB17 .A26 2019 (print) | DDC 943.6--dc23
LC record available at https://lccn.loc.gov/2018007568

Printed in the United States of America

Cover images
Main: *Salzburg.*
Left: *Apple Strudel.*
Center: *Statue* of *Johann Strauss*
Right: *A walker in the Alps.*

QR CODES AND LINKS TO THIRD-PARTY CONTENT

You may gain access to certain third-party content ("Third- Party Sites") by scanning and using the QR Codes that appear in this publication (the "QR Codes"). We do not operate or control in any respect any information, products, or services on such Third-Party Sites linked to by us via the QR Codes included in this publication, and we assume no responsibility for any materials you may access using the QR Codes. Your use of the QR Codes may be subject to terms, limitations, or restrictions set forth in the applicable terms of use or otherwise established by the owners of the Third-Party Sites. Our linking to such Third-Party Sites via the QR Codes does not imply an endorsement or sponsorship of such Third-Party Sites or the information, products, or services offered on or through the Third-Party Sites, nor does it imply an endorsement or sponsorship of this publication by the owners of such Third-Party Sites.

CONTENTS

Austria at a Glance	6
Chapter 1: Austria's Geography & Landscape	11
Chapter 2: The Government & History of Austria	23
Chapter 3: The Austrian Economy	43
Chapter 4: Citizens of Austria: People, Customs & Culture	53
Chapter 5: The Famous Cities of Austria	67
Chapter 6: A Bright Future for Austria	81
Chronology	90
Further Reading & Internet Resources	91
Index	92
Picture Credits & Author	96

KEY ICONS TO LOOK FOR:

Words to Understand: These words with their easy-to-understand definitions will increase the reader's understanding of the text while building vocabulary skills.

Sidebars: This boxed material within the main text allows readers to build knowledge, gain insights, explore possibilities, and broaden their perspectives by weaving together additional information to provide realistic and holistic perspectives.

Educational Videos: Readers can view videos by scanning our QR codes, providing them with additional content to supplement the text. Examples include news coverage, moments in history, speeches, iconic sports moments, and much more!

Text-Dependent Questions: These questions send the reader back to the text for more careful attention to the evidence presented there.

Research Projects: Readers are pointed toward areas of further inquiry connected to each chapter. Suggestions are provided for projects that encourage deeper research and analysis.

AUSTRIA AT A GLANCE

MAP OF EUROPE

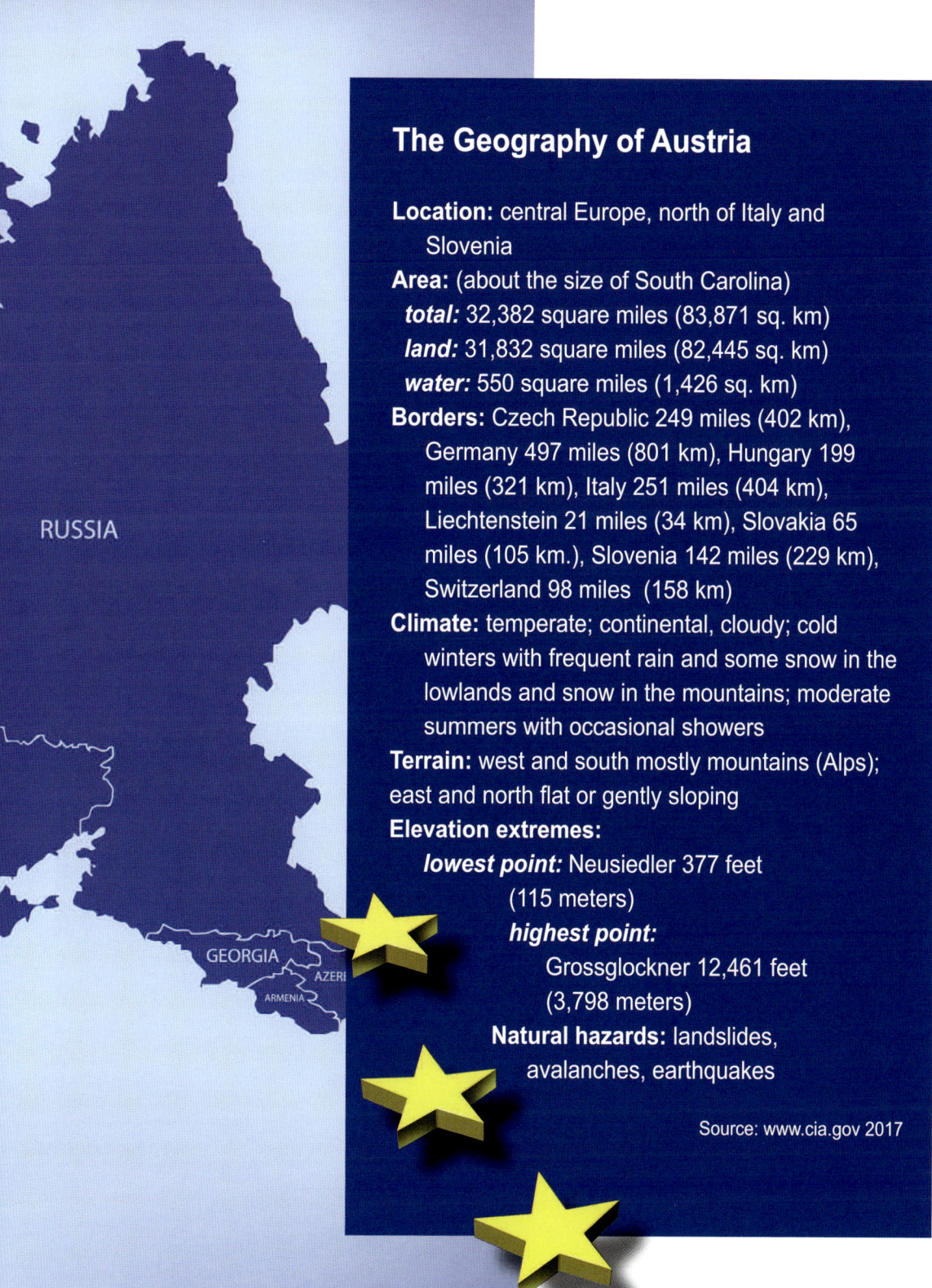

The Geography of Austria

Location: central Europe, north of Italy and Slovenia

Area: (about the size of South Carolina)
  total: 32,382 square miles (83,871 sq. km)
  land: 31,832 square miles (82,445 sq. km)
  water: 550 square miles (1,426 sq. km)

Borders: Czech Republic 249 miles (402 km), Germany 497 miles (801 km), Hungary 199 miles (321 km), Italy 251 miles (404 km), Liechtenstein 21 miles (34 km), Slovakia 65 miles (105 km.), Slovenia 142 miles (229 km), Switzerland 98 miles (158 km)

Climate: temperate; continental, cloudy; cold winters with frequent rain and some snow in the lowlands and snow in the mountains; moderate summers with occasional showers

Terrain: west and south mostly mountains (Alps); east and north flat or gently sloping

Elevation extremes:
  lowest point: Neusiedler 377 feet (115 meters)
  highest point: Grossglockner 12,461 feet (3,798 meters)
  Natural hazards: landslides, avalanches, earthquakes

Source: www.cia.gov 2017

AUSTRIA AT A GLANCE

Flag of Austria

Austria is predominantly a country of mountains and forests, with permanent snow and glaciers on the higher areas. Most of its population lives in the east. Austria is a neutral country as pledged by law and treaties after World War II, but it joined the European Union in 1995. It was occupied by the Germans in 1938, and then by the Allies in 1945, and the modern state did not regain full independence until 1955. The flag dates back to 1191 and the Siege of Acre during the Third Crusade, when it is said that the only part of Duke Leopold V's tunic not bloodstained was beneath his swordbelt. The design was officially adopted in 1918 with the dissolution of the Austro-Hungarian Empire, although the colors had been in use since 1230.

ABOVE: The Naschmarkt is a popular market in Vienna that dates back to the sixteenth century. It is famous for its wine bars, cafés, and restaurants.

EUROPEAN COUNTRIES TODAY: AUSTRIA

The People of Austria

Population: 8,711,770 (July 2016 est.)
Ethnic Groups: Austrians 91.1%, former Yugoslavs 4% (includes Croatians, Slovenes, Serbs, and Bosniaks), Turks 1.6%, German 0.9%, other or unspecified 2.4% (last census)
Age Structure:
    0–14 years: 14.02%
    15–24 years: 11.33%
    25–54 years: 42.71%
    55–64 years: 12.85%
    65 years and above: 19.09%
Population Growth Rate: 0.51% (2016 est.)
Birth Rate: 9.5 births/1,000 population (2016 est.)
Death Rate: 9.5 deaths/1,000 population (July 2016 est.)
Migration Rate: 5.2 migrant(s)/1,000 population (2016 est.)
Infant Mortality Rate: 3.4 deaths/1,000 live births
Life Expectancy at Birth:
Total Population: 81.5 years
    Male: 78.9 years
    Female: 84.3 years (2016 est.)
Total Fertility Rate: 1.47 children born/woman (2016 est.)
Religions: Catholic 73.8%, Protestant 4.9%, Muslim 4.2%, Orthodox 2.2%, other 0.8%, none 12%, unspecified 2%
Languages: German 73.6%, Turkish 4.%, Serbian 4.2%, Croatian 3.5%, Slovene 2%, Hungarian 12% (last census)
Literacy rate: 98%

Source: www.cia.gov 2017

Words to Understand

bisect: To cut or divide into two parts, especially two equal parts.

deciduous: The shedding of leaves seasonally by various species of trees and shrubs.

precipitation: Rain, snow, sleet, or hail that falls to the ground.

BELOW: The Pinzgauer is a breed of domestic cattle from the Pinzgau region of Austria. It is known for its distinctive brown and white markings.

Chapter One
AUSTRIA'S GEOGRAPHY & LANDSCAPE

Austria is a relatively small country, covering about 32,382 square miles (83,871 square kilometers). This may seem large, but consider the fact that the whole country is about the size of South Carolina. Austria is completely surrounded by land; it shares borders with eight different countries: Switzerland, Liechtenstein, Germany, Czech Republic, Slovakia, Hungary, Slovenia, and Italy.

A Country Covered with Mountains

Austria is one of the most mountainous countries in the world, with more than 80 percent of its surface covered with mountain ranges. It has an average elevation of 3,000 feet (910 meters). The highest mountain in the country is the Grossglockner, which is about 12,500 feet tall (3,798 meters). This is taller than four Empire State buildings stacked on top of each other! Wide valleys intersect these peaks, creating many different geographic areas. The first of these is the Alps, famous for skiing. The Alpine region includes mountains from the west to the south. This famous mountain range has a high amount of **precipitation**, along with short summers and long winters. In the valleys, the air is warm and dry. From twenty to forty days a year these valleys experience a dry wind called *föhn*. This is most common in the spring and fall and it can be dangerous, since the force of the wind can cause large rocks to fall off the faces of the mountains, leading to avalanches. The wind is so dry that it also leads to a high probability of fires. The winters in this area are long and the summers short.

   The second geographic region is in southeast Austria, which contains sheltered valleys that are quite a bit warmer than their Alpine counterparts. This leads to an earlier spring, but winter is still just as harsh as in the mountains—

AUSTRIA'S GEOGRAPHY & LANDSCAPE

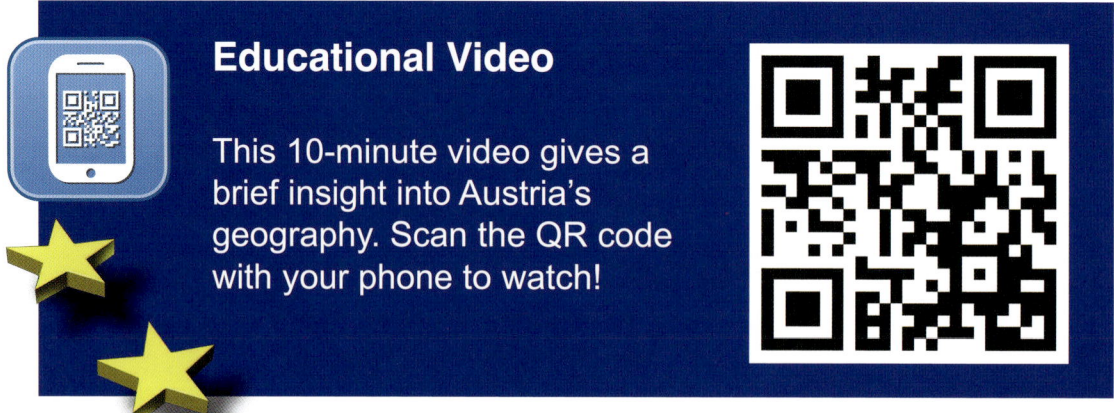

about 4°F (-15°C). The weather here is characterized by frequent heavy thunderstorms.

To the northeast and east lie the respective Vienna and Danube basins, Austria's driest areas. Because the air is so dry, they rarely receive a deep snowfall, but what snow there is can last four weeks during the cold winters. The summers are warm but not hot, with an average of about 68°F (20°C). If you don't like cool weather, Austria is not the country for you!

Bodies of Water

While it has many rivers and lakes, Austria's most important body of water is the Danube River, which is 217.4 miles (350 kilometers) long. This waterway **bisects** the northern section of the country as it flows from west to east. The Danube is an important means of transportation and has been the focus of songs and stories throughout history, notably the "Blue Danube" waltz by Johann Strauss.

Austria has many lakes within its borders. One of these is Lake Neusiedl, a bird haven home to many unique species. Another is Lake Langbathsee, which is surrounded by scenery so picturesque that in prior times, Emperor Franz Josef built a summer lodge here. The Attersee is the largest lake in Austria, followed by the Traunsee. These large, deep lakes are cooler than the rest, and their water is of a better quality for drinking.

EUROPEAN COUNTRIES TODAY: AUSTRIA

Vegetation

Austria is one of Europe's most heavily wooded countries, and because of its varied climate, it has many types of plants. The vegetation varies from deciduous forests to mixed forests with trees like beech and fir. At higher altitudes, one can see trees such as fir, larch, and pine. The northern edge of the Alps is mostly grassland, while to the east are many plants found only on the salt steppes east of Lake Neusiedl.

ABOVE: *A rare flat area in Austria, Lake Neusiedl is a haven for birdlife including rare birds.*

AUSTRIA'S GEOGRAPHY & LANDSCAPE

Alpine Plants

Alpine plants grow in an alpine climate and therefore are suited to the mountainous regions of Austria. While hardy, they usually have very beautiful flowers. Over thousands of years, they have evolved to cope with the extreme cold, heat, and dryness of the mountain peaks. Alpines consist of many different species, including: perennial grasses, sedges, forbs, cushion plants, mosses, and lichens. Austria's national flower, edelweiss (above right), is an alpine belonging to the daisy family.

Many types of plants grow only on the mountains, some of which are alpine plants. Although they only bloom for a short period, the sight of them is beautiful. In order to survive at very high altitudes, they have adapted over time to cope with the conditions.

Austrians have set aside 3 percent of their country for parks. These preserves protect unique and endangered plants that cannot be found anywhere else. The national parks include rain forests, as well as virgin forests, that have grown for thousands of years, untouched by human activity.

Wildlife

The animals that live in Austria are more or less native to all of Europe. They include deer, marmot, fox, badger, and marten. The Alpine regions have different species of wildlife, such as chamois—which is like a cross between a goat and an antelope—groundhog, eagle, and mountain jackdaw.

EUROPEAN COUNTRIES TODAY: AUSTRIA

ABOVE: *Campanula (Bellflower) is adapted to growing at high altitudes.*

AUSTRIA'S GEOGRAPHY & LANDSCAPE

ABOVE: *The majestic golden eagle is native to the mountainous regions of Austria.*

EUROPEAN COUNTRIES TODAY: AUSTRIA

Eurasian Lynx

The Eurasian or European lynx is a medium-sized cat native to Europe. It is the third-largest predator after the brown bear and gray wolf. It is the largest of the four lynx species and a strict carnivore, consuming two or three pounds (one or two kg) of meat every day. This extremely efficient hunter uses fine-tuned stealth and pounce techniques to bring down animals four times its size, delivering a fatal bite to the neck or snout of an unsuspecting deer. During winter, its variably patterned coat is long and dense and large fur-covered paws help it move through deep snow. The Eurasian lynx is an endangered species. It can be found in Austria, but in small numbers. Its main threat is hunting and habitat loss.

Source: http://www.bbc.co.uk/nature/life/Eurasian_Lynx

There is also a vast bird population in the reed beds of Lake Neusiedl (heron, spoonbill, scooper, wild goose, and many more).

Austria is also home to many endangered species, such as the Eurasian brown bear and lynx. The golden and wood grouse are protected but not yet endangered. Austria has also helped with the reintroduction of species. For example, the ibex and wild boar have both been reintroduced to the wild, and their populations are gradually increasing.

Austria's rich natural resources have played their part in the land's history. Its land and its long historical heritage have helped shape the modern nation and its government.

AUSTRIA'S GEOGRAPHY & LANDSCAPE

Austria's National Parks

Austria's national parks stretch across almost 3 percent of the country. Each park has its own unique natural landscape, flora, and fauna. Austria's most important and pristine natural landscapes are protected within these parks.

Neusiedler See-Seewinkel

The Neusiedler See-Seewinkel National Park has a distinctive steppe landscape. It is one of the most fascinating natural environments in Europe, featuring reed beds, marsh meadows, and saltwater lakes. Most of the lake is surrounded by reeds, which serve as a habitat for wildlife. The area is home to some 340 bird species and notable other species such as the Balkan frog and the Danube warty newt. The lake's shores form one of the most important birdwatching sanctuaries in Europe.

Donau-Auen

Central Europe's largest continuous landscape of riverside meadows serves as an ideal habitat for some 5,000 animal species. The unspoiled natural paradise of the Donau-Auen National Park is right on the doorstep of Vienna, providing a fascinating recreational area for those who want to explore the countryside on foot and marvel at its tranquil natural beauty.

Thayatal

Over thousands of years, the river Thaya has created a valley landscape of great beauty. Due to its wonderful natural attractions, the area was declared a national park at the beginning of 2000. The meadows, wooded hillsides, cliffs, and stretches of grassland provide habitats for numerous rare animals and plant species, including: the eagle owl, black stork, green lizard, fraxinella, and colored iris. The valley's unique charm is perhaps best experienced at the "Umlaufberg," a narrow ridge of rock that separates the two sections of the river. Another highlight of Thayatal National Park is its wealth of castles and ruined fortresses, many of which have interesting legends that have grown up around them.

EUROPEAN COUNTRIES TODAY: AUSTRIA

ABOVE: Hardegg Castle in the Thaya valley in Thayatal National Park.

Hohe Tauern
Central Europe's largest area of protected landscape extends over three Austrian provinces: Tirol, Carinthia, and Salzburg. It is a region of ancient forests, lush green alpine pastures, rugged mountainsides, and spectacular waterfalls. It is a mountainous area with more than a hundred peaks and has a great diversity of alpine flora and fauna.

Kalkalpen
Kalkalpen National Park is home to the largest uninterrupted forest in Austria. Spruce, fir, and beech trees cover four-fifths of the terrain. The trees are left to grow, mature, and then die naturally. The fallen trees are an important habitat for countless species, ranging from beetles to woodpeckers. While the new generation of trees grows, insects and microorganisms breakdown the remains

AUSTRIA'S GEOGRAPHY & LANDSCAPE

of the fallen trees to produce fertile soil. Apart from the fascinating flora and fauna, there are also spectacular canyons and gorges, picturesque waterfalls, and lakes.

Gesäuse

Austria's third largest and newest park, characterized by steep mountain slopes and gorges in a valley formed by the river Enns. The altitude ranges from 1,607 feet (490 meters) up to 7,775 feet (2,370 meters) at the peak of the Hochtor. It

ABOVE: *Weißsee, "White Lake" in Hohe Tauern National Park.*

EUROPEAN COUNTRIES TODAY: AUSTRIA

is a natural habitat for 90 species of breeding birds, marmots, chamois, and deer, plus around 50 different types of wild orchid.

Nockberge Biosphere Reserve
The Nockberge Biosphere Reserve is Europe's only high mountain national park, and it boasts the East Alps' largest pine, larch, and spruce forest. The distinctive shape of the gently rolling Nockberge Mountains is interesting geologically and unique to the Alps. The mountains were formed some hundred million years ago by an interchange of lands, seas, deserts, and jungles. This pristine mountain landscape with its soft hills and endless pastures is so exceptional that it was designated a conservation area in 1987.

Text-Dependent Questions

1. When was Austria occupied by Germany?

2. What is Austria's national flower?

3. What is the name of Austria's most important river?

Research Project

Select five plant species and five animal species that live in the Alps and explain how they have adapted to the harsh Alpine conditions.

21

Words to Understand

Bohemia: A historical region and former kingdom of the present-day western Czech Republic.

empire: A group of states or countries ruled over by a single sovereign authority.

treaty: A formally concluded and ratified agreement between states.

BELOW: Schönbühel Castle on the Danube River stands on the edge of a high and uneven cliff in the Austrian valley of Wachau.

Chapter Two
THE GOVERNMENT & HISTORY OF AUSTRIA

Austria has been populated for thousands of years; evidence has been found that shows humans have lived in the area since the Paleolithic Age (about 80,000 to 10,000 BCE). For instance, in 1991, the mummy of a man dating back to the Stone Age was found in the ice of the Alps, almost perfectly preserved. Later on, from about 800 to 400 BCE, many Celtic tribes inhabited Austria, trading with others from all over Europe. This was a period when many groups invaded the land, partly because of the availability and convenience of the Danube River. These tribes included the Celts, as well as Romans and others.

The Roman Empire

The Romans founded Vienna, now the capital of Austria. They settled many other towns as well, and in the second century CE brought about the spread of Christianity to the region.

When the Roman Empire lost power around 470 CE, the Roman culture that had permeated the area disappeared. From

ABOVE: *Charlemagne by Albrecht Dürer.*

THE GOVERNMENT & HISTORY OF AUSTRIA

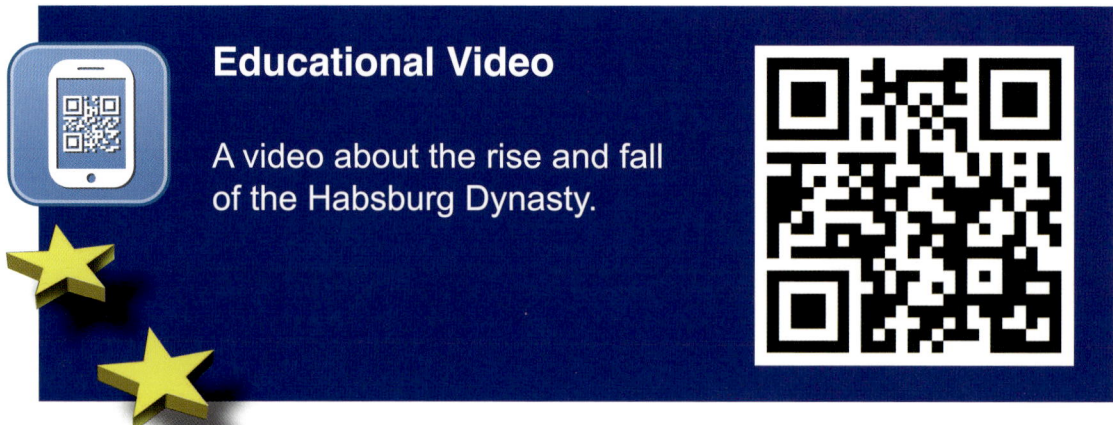

Educational Video

A video about the rise and fall of the Habsburg Dynasty.

this point on, Austria was prey to many wandering tribes and armies. Then, in the eighth century, Charlemagne established the territory as part of his Holy Roman Empire. This lasted until his death in 907, after which anarchy reigned until Otto the Great conquered the area in 955.

The Babenberg Dynasty

After that era, which lasted about twenty years, a new family took control. These were the Babenbergs, whose rule lasted for more than three centuries. They were the ones who gave the region its name: Österreich or Austria.

In the thirteenth century, however, the emperor of the Holy Roman Empire invaded Austria. He refused to recognize the rule of the Babenberg king, and both sides fought. King Ottokar was killed on the battlefield and Emperor Rudolf von Habsburg took control, starting a dynasty that would last more than 600 years.

Habsburg Rule

The Habsburgs expanded their territory; over time, the family controlled land in **Bohemia**, Spain, and Hungary, as well as Austria. The empire was forced to divide because of its great size-eventually, there were two branches: one controlling the area around Austria and Germany, the other in charge of Spain and Holland. However, this power would not last forever.

24

EUROPEAN COUNTRIES TODAY: AUSTRIA

ABOVE: *Emperor Rudolf II by Hans von Aachen.*

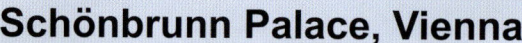

Schönbrunn Palace, Vienna

Its great size notwithstanding, the Schönbrunn Palace is not an intimidating building. That may be due partly to its mellow golden color and the arrangement of the facade, in which the broad wings are brought forward in a welcoming manner. A third reason is the absence of the three imposing domes that the architect, Johann Fischer von Erlach, placed over the main entrance, though their removal plays havoc with the general proportions.

On the outskirts of Vienna, the Schönbrunn was the summer palace of the Habsburgs during roughly the last third of their 600-year reign in Austria. A hunting lodge stood here, where the Emperor Maximilian had his menagerie in the early sixteenth century; there is still a zoo, founded in 1752, and it is one of the oldest in Europe. The house was destroyed during the siege of Vienna by the Turks in 1683, but the Emperor Leopold nevertheless decided to replace it with a palace on a grand scale. Fischer von Erlach was then approaching the height of his fame, but his original design of 1690, which aimed to challenge Versailles, was rejected as too costly even for the Habsburgs. A second plan was put into effect in 1696 and the building was largely completed by 1711. It was subsequently modified somewhat, first by Fischer von Erlach's son, Josef Emanuel, and again by Nikolaus Pacassi, who removed the domes in 1744. Probably its most famous resident was the Empress Maria Theresa, who spent nearly every summer of her reign (1740–80) here. The palace and grounds were first opened to the public in 1918.

The Schönbrunn contains an alleged 1,440 rooms, most of them of an ornate magnificence that is striking even by the standards of Austrian Baroque. Among the showpieces are the Great Gallery, with its staggering painted ceiling, huge chandeliers, and inlaid floor, the adjoining Hall of Ceremonies, and the sparkling Hall of Mirrors. Smaller rooms, such as the Yellow Drawing Room, are equally splendid in their way and, being on a more human scale, perhaps more attractive to the modern visitor.

THE GOVERNMENT & HISTORY OF AUSTRIA

While the Habsburg rulers were busy expanding their territory, they were ignoring the potential threat of the Ottomans. This group gained in power, and in 1453, they took control of Constantinople, the capital of the Holy Roman Empire. Twice they were able to invade far as Vienna, but both times they met fierce resistance at the city limits. Finally, under Prince Eugene of Savoy, the Habsburg army was able to rid the country of the Turks and take back their territory.

Protestantism

Although seemingly peaceful now, the empire still had problems to face. As economies based on currency spread, the importance of Austrian trade routes decreased. Because of economic and political instability, the Protestant Revolution spread rapidly in Austria. The Habsburgs tried to undo the results of this spread of Protestantism through the Counter Revolution. This alliance between the Austrian government and the Catholic Church continued throughout the rule of the Habsburg dynasty.

ABOVE: *Archduke Ferdinand II by Francesco Terzi.*

At first, it was impossible to keep the Protestants from practicing their religion, and so the rulers of Austria opted for a policy of toleration. However, under Ferdinand II, strong feelings against Protestants led to the Thirty Years' War (1618–48). After the war ended with the Peace of Westphalia, the Habsburg lands became their own empire, separate from the Holy Roman Empire, which gradually lost power and faded into the background.

In 1700, the last Spanish Habsburg died. This caused clashes between governments as many countries tried to win control of Spain. Austria lost this War of Spanish Succession, but it was able to keep control of its territories in Italy and the Netherlands.

EUROPEAN COUNTRIES TODAY: AUSTRIA

At this time, the monarchy was not absolute. In other words, it left many rights to the provinces, such as taxation. However, other powers still rested in the hands of the emperor, including the repression of free speech and worship.

Maria Theresa: The First Queen of Austria

In 1740, Emperor Karl VI died without any male heirs. Thus, out of necessity, the crown passed to his daughter, Maria Theresa. The new empress was forced to prove herself in more than one war as she fought off those who yearned after her lands, like the Prussian king Friedrich II. Throughout both the Silesian War (1740–48) and the Seven Years' War (1756–63), she managed to keep her territory together. The only province she lost was Silesia, which she gave up to Prussia.

ABOVE: *Maria Theresa by Martin van Meytens.*

Maria Theresa's husband was later elected emperor of the Holy Roman Empire. However, he was never as successful as the strong woman he married. She and her son Joseph II put into place many reforms that are still important today, including the abolition of serfdom and the secularization of monasteries and other church lands.

The French Revolution Brings New Ideas

This peaceful age of monarchs lasted until the 1790s when the French Revolution brought ideas of equality and democracy to Austria. Threatened by these new ideals, Emperor Franz II, the grandson of Maria Theresa and the nephew of the French queen Marie Antoinette (who was beheaded during the

THE GOVERNMENT & HISTORY OF AUSTRIA

ABOVE: *Francis (Franz) II, Holy Roman Emperor by Friedrich von Amerling.*

revolution), took action. He joined a coalition against France. This might have seemed like a good idea at the time, but Austria later suffered great losses under the invasion of Napoleon Bonaparte.

The two countries became involved in a power struggle. Napoleon crowned himself emperor of France in 1804, and Franz followed his example by creating the Empire of Austria. In 1806, the Holy Roman Empire dissolved because of the Confederation of the Rhine—a group of fifteen German states that joined with France. Therefore, Franz was forced to give up his crown. From then on, Napoleon was able to inflict heavy losses on Austria. He even went so far as to conquer Vienna twice. However, he, like all other men, was not indestructible. He was finally defeated at Waterloo and was exiled to the island of Saint Helen, where he died in 1821. The old order of monarchies was restored in Europe.

The Monarchy Weakens

Early in 1848, the idea of freedom for the middle classes again reached Austria from France. This time the people asked for freedom of the press as well as a constitution. The hated police system of the time was swept away, but the remainder of the revolution was stopped.

ABOVE: Napoleon Bonaparte by Jacques Louis David.

THE GOVERNMENT & HISTORY OF AUSTRIA

Emperor Franz Joseph I put into place a system that left no room for anything except the absolute right of a monarch to rule.

Because of his rule and policy of neutrality, especially during the Crimean War (1854–56), Austria found itself without friends or allies when it was attacked by Sardinia. Three years later, Austria was forced to give up its territory of Lombardy. With the October Diploma and the February Edict, the country also put in place a parliament.

The government was weakening, and reorganization was needed. In 1867, a compromise was reached that put in place a dual state: the Austro-Hungarian Empire. A cultural minority ruled the people, making other groups, especially the Slavs, unhappy.

Around this time, two political parties—the Social Democratic Party and the Christian Social Party—emerged. Both demanded civil rights for the people and were able to let their voices be heard in Austria's first general election in 1907. Anti-Semitism also spread at this time as many poor Jews moved to Austria from the eastern provinces of the empire. Despite these setbacks, some aspects of the culture flourished, and Vienna becoming a major center of the arts.

Austria was relatively peaceful from this time until the beginning of World War I. It had learned from its previous mistakes and formed alliances with other countries, including the German Empire and Italy, together with which it formed the Triple Alliance. However, feelings of nationalism grew, causing tensions to rise. People also demanded better pay and working conditions, setting the stage for World War I to begin.

World War I

On June 28, 1914, Archduke Franz Ferdinand was assassinated. He was the heir to the Austro-Hungarian throne, and his murder by a member of a nationalist group caused the regional tensions that had been building for years to flare into a full-fledged war.

The first three years of fighting were futile; none of the European nations emerged with a clear lead. The entrance of the United States into World War I in 1917 helped tip the scales against the Central Powers (Austria-Hungary, the German Empire, and Turkey). After the war ended, the Austro-

EUROPEAN COUNTRIES TODAY: AUSTRIA

ABOVE: *Archduke Franz Ferdinand, his wife Sophie, and their children.*

THE GOVERNMENT & HISTORY OF AUSTRIA

Hungarian Empire dissolved into small nation states, one of which later formed the Republic of Austria.

In 1919, at the end of the war, the Treaty of Saint-Germain established fixed borders for Austria. It also made sure that the new country was forbidden to form any alliances with Germany. In the end, Austria was a small country of about 7 million people, more than a third of whom lived in Vienna. Whereas the empire had been self-sufficient, now Austria was forced to look elsewhere for raw materials, food, and markets for its goods. Because of this, the economy crashed and a period of starvation ensued. Inflation set in, which was only stopped when the League of Nations (a precursor to the United Nations) stepped in and helped.

Socialism in Austria

The postwar country's political views swerved as far from monarchy as is possible. Two socialist factions, the "Red," who were more moderate, and the "Black," who believed that the clergy should have more power, headed the new socialist views. Conflict escalated between the two groups when the Black won the 1921 election, and riots raged in the streets of Vienna. In the end, two private militias both posed a threat to the government. Eventually, the National Socialist Party (the Black) gained popularity, partly because of the increase in anti-Semitism.

A new chancellor, Engelbert Dollfus, came into power in 1932. He was against National Socialism; however, he believed in fascism. Because of this, Dollfus quickly became involved with Mussolini, the Italian fascist leader of the time. Because Dollfus was so

ABOVE: Chancellor Engelbert Dollfus in 1933.

EUROPEAN COUNTRIES TODAY: AUSTRIA

suppressive of the socialists, a revolt occurred in 1934, but the army soon put it down. After this demonstration, all political parties were banned, and a totalitarian state was put into place. Dollfus was assassinated in 1934.

At this time, German influence, led by Adolph Hitler, increased in Austria. The new chancellor, Kurt von Schuschnigg, appointed the National Socialists to government posts. Finally, Hitler forced Schuschnigg to resign, and Austria was occupied by German troops in 1938.

After World War II, when Germany was vanquished, Austria regained its freedom when the Allies decided to reestablish Austria as an independent nation. In 1945, it was taken over by Soviet and American troops and a provisional government was set in place. The original constitution was restored with one major revision: the country was now divided into separate occupation zones, each controlled by a different Allied power.

Reconstruction

Now began the job of reconstructing the economy and the government. However, recovery didn't go as fast as was expected because of the decline of trade between the two halves of Europe. Eastern Europe remained communist, with tension between it and democratic Western Europe. Finally, in 1955, a formal treaty between France, Great Britain, the United States, the USSR (the Soviets), and Austria put the Austrian government back in the hands of its native citizens. There was a heavy price, though: Austria had to pay reparations to the USSR, as well as promise to remain neutral in all future conflicts and to never purchase or develop weapons of mass destruction. After this treaty was passed, Austria was allowed into the United Nations.

ABOVE: *11th Chancellor Kurt von Schuschnigg.*

35

THE GOVERNMENT & HISTORY OF AUSTRIA

By the 1960s, Austria was back on its feet. The country had joined the European Free Trade Association in 1959, allowing it to trade without having to pay tariffs to the other European nations. The balance of power between the liberals and the conservatives was about equal, with both the People's Party and the Socialists maintaining control at various times.

Modern Government

In 1983, the Socialist government fell, and it joined forces with the radical Freedom Party. Three years later, Kurt Waldheim was elected president, despite rumors he had been involved in atrocities as a German officer during World War II. His election caused controversy throughout the world.

By the late 1980s, Austria had become more capitalist as it started to privatize some state-owned industries. In 1995, it entered the European Union (EU).

Today, Austria's government has many parties. The three most well known are the People's Party, the Social Democrats, and the Freedom Party, which is far right and radical. In 2017, the People's Party and Freedom Party joined together, in a coalition, so that a stable government could be formed, but this led to Austria being criticized by the rest of the EU because of the radical

Austrian Parliament

The Austrian Parliament (German: *Österreichisches Parlament*) consists of two chambers: the National Council (*Nationalrat*) and the Federal Council (*Bundesrat*). In specific cases, both houses convene as the Federal Assembly (*Bundesversammlung*). All houses convene in the Austrian Parliament Building in Vienna.

EUROPEAN COUNTRIES TODAY: AUSTRIA

ABOVE: *The Austrian Parliament Building, Vienna, was completed in 1883.*

THE GOVERNMENT & HISTORY OF AUSTRIA

ABOVE: *The modern complex of Donau City, Vienna.*

EUROPEAN COUNTRIES TODAY: AUSTRIA

Freedom Party's involvement in the government. The leader of the People's Party's, Sebastian Kurz, at 31 became the world's youngest head of government. Unlike most of Europe's populist parties, the Freedom Party managed to translate its success at the ballot box into real political power. The deal made Austria the only Western European state with a governing far-right party, which is opposed to migration and the European Union.

Austria's current president is independent candidate Alexander Van der Bellen, who assumed office in 2017.

The Power of Young Voters

Austria's politics are increasingly influenced by Austrian youth. In 2007, all Austrians sixteen or older gained the right to vote.

Text-Dependent Questions

1. Why did the Babenburg dynasty come to an end?

2. How long did Habsburg rule last?

3. Who is Austria's current president?

Research Project

Using internet resources for research, compare and contrast each of Austria's political parties.

THE GOVERNMENT & HISTORY OF AUSTRIA

The Formation of the European Union (EU)

The EU is a confederation of European nations that continues to grow. As of 2017, there are twenty-eight official members. Several other candidates are also waiting for approval. All countries that enter the EU agree to follow common laws about foreign security policies. They also agree to cooperate on legal matters that go on within the EU. The European Council meets to discuss all international matters and make decisions about them. Each country's own concerns and interests are important, though. And apart from legal and financial issues, the EU tries to uphold values such as peace, human dignity, freedom, and equality.

All member countries remain autonomous. This means that they generally keep their own laws and regulations. The idea for a union among European nations was first mentioned after World War II. The war had devastated much of Europe, both physically and financially. In 1950, the French foreign minister suggested that France and West Germany combine their coal and steel industries under one authority. Both countries would have control over the

ABOVE: *The entrance to the European Union Parliament Building in Brussels.*

EUROPEAN COUNTRIES TODAY: AUSTRIA

Member Countries

Austria	Greece	Romania
Belgium	Hungary	Slovakia
Bulgaria	Ireland	Slovenia
Croatia	Italy	Spain
Cyprus	Latvia	Sweden
Czech Republic	Lithuania	United Kingdom
Denmark	Luxembourg	*(Brexit: For the time*
Estonia	Malta	*being, the United*
Finland	Netherlands	*Kingdom remains a full*
France	Poland	*member of the EU.)*
Germany	Portugal	

industries. This would help them become more financially stable. It would also make war between the countries much more difficult. The idea was interesting to other European countries as well. In 1951, France, West Germany, Belgium, Luxembourg, the Netherlands, and Italy signed the Treaty of Paris, creating the European Coal and Steel Community. These six countries would become the core of the EU.

In 1957, these same countries signed the Treaties of Rome, creating the European Economic Community. In 1965, the Merger Treaty formed the European Community. Finally, in 1992, the Maastricht Treaty was signed. This treaty defined the European Union. It gave a framework for expanding the EU's political role, particularly in the area of foreign and security policy. It would also replace national currencies with the euro. The next year, the treaty went into effect. At that time, the member countries included the original six plus another six who had joined during the 1970s and '80s.

In the following years, the EU would take more steps to form a single market for its members. This would make joining the union even more advantageous. In addition to enlargement, the EU is steadily becoming more integrated through its own policies for closer cooperation between member states.

Words to Understand

GDP: Gross Domestic Product. The value of a country's overall output of goods and services.

privatize: The transfer of a business, industry, or service from public to private ownership and control.

hydroelectric: The generation of electricity using flowing water, typically from a reservoir held behind a dam or other barrier.

BELOW: Austria has an important winemaking industry. Various wines are produced, mainly in the east of the country.

Chapter Three
THE AUSTRIAN ECONOMY

After World War II, the government took control of many of Austria's industries to prevent them from coming under the control of the USSR for the payment of war reparations. Because of this, for a long time the government had a large role in the economy. In the past twenty years, however, the country has started to **privatize** businesses. This process has largely been successful, but the government still owns some industries and services. Despite being in the middle of changing hands, Austria's economy is very strong for various reasons. One of these is that now, as throughout history,

ABOVE: *The oil refinery at Schwechat is owned by the Austrian Mineral Oil Administration.*

THE AUSTRIAN ECONOMY

ABOVE: The Mooser Dam, high up in the mountains near Kaprun, produces hydroelectricity.

EUROPEAN COUNTRIES TODAY: AUSTRIA

Austrian Crystal

Austrian crystal is man-made, essentially by cutting hand-blown glass into beautiful, sparkling objects. Austria's largest producer and exporter is Swarovski, who operate from their headquarter in Wattens. They manufacture hundreds of different items, ranging from watches, jewlery, chandeliers, and other pieces, all adorned with the highest quality of crystals. Their products are sold all over the world. Swarovski crystals are also manufactured for optical devices, computers, and for heavy duty cutting machinery.

Austria serves as a hub between many countries. Goods flow through the country, especially fuels like oil and natural gas.

Austria's geographical position within Europe makes it a convenient site for countless treaty meetings and international conferences. Each time this happens, business is brought into the country from international sources, helping the economy.

The Austrian government places a great emphasis on aiding the poor and less fortunate, and strives for a fair society. Austria is known for its enviable social security system that supports the whole Austrian population.

Industries

Austria is highly industrialized and makes such goods as vehicle engines and other electronic parts like airbag chips and braking systems for cars. However, the country is also known for the high percentage of its people who are employed not by giant corporations but by smaller companies. For example, many are involved in the craft-making industry. Austria is famous for handmade items like jewelry, ceramics, and blown glass. Tourism also contributes to the country's Gross Domestic Product (**GDP**), as people from all over the world visit this beautiful country.

THE AUSTRIAN ECONOMY

While much of the economy consists of smaller businesses, there are some large industries like iron and steel processing plants, as well as a large chemical manufacturing business. Other goods that are manufactured in Austria are lumber and processed wood (such as paper); computers and other communication equipment; and machinery.

Part of the reason that Austria is so prosperous is the abundance of raw materials from which the country can draw. The land is rich with deposits of iron and other important minerals buried deep below the earth's surface. Austria also has its own sources of oil and natural gas. As scientists work to end the world's dependence on oil, Austria is now generating **hydroelectric** power and is now the country that supplies the most to other members of the EU.

ABOVE: *Mozart's house in Salzburg is a popular tourist attraction. Tourism in Austria brings in much revenue for the economy.*

Educational Video

This film showcases Austria's economic strengths and its export companies. With music and images.

EUROPEAN COUNTRIES TODAY: AUSTRIA

ABOVE: Austria's winter sports industry is very important to its economy.

THE AUSTRIAN ECONOMY

Imports and Exports

Altogether, Austria trades with over 150 countries; the member countries in the EU account for more than two-thirds of all exports. Most of these goods go to Germany, Italy, France, Switzerland, and Czech Republic. Austria also trades with the United States. The country exports such things as machinery, motor vehicles, paper, chemicals, iron, fabrics, and food.

In return for these goods, Austria receives many others. These include chemicals, metal goods, oil, and mechanical equipment. Many of the goods are the same as those they import, and while this might seem redundant, there is a reason. When a country produces a good, they are also using up resources

ABOVE: *Austrian food is similar to the produce of other nearby countries such as Italy, Hungary, and Germany. This Austrian market is displaying food typical to Austria.*

EUROPEAN COUNTRIES TODAY: AUSTRIA

The Economy of Austria

Gross Domestic Product (GDP): $417.1 billion (2016 est.)
GDP Per Capita: $47,900 (2016 est.)
Industries: construction, machinery, vehicles and parts, food, metals, chemicals, lumber and wood processing, paper and paperboard, communications equipment, tourism
Agriculture: grains, potatoes, wine, fruit, dairy products, cattle, pigs, poultry, lumber
Export Commodities: machinery and equipment, motor vehicles and parts, paper and paperboard, metal goods, chemicals, iron and steel, textiles, foodstuffs
Export Partners: Germany 30.5%, Italy 7.9%, US 6.6%, Switzerland 5.5%, France 4.1%, Czech Republic 4.1% (2015)
Import Commodities: machinery and equipment, motor vehicles, chemicals, metal goods, oil and oil products; foodstuffs
Import Partners: Germany 37.2%, Italy 6.2%, China 5.9%, Switzerland 5.3% Czech Republic 4.3% (2015)
Currency: euro

Source: www.cia.gov 2017

that might have been used in making different goods. Most of the time countries manufacture goods with the least production costs; this allows them to make as many things as possible. However, sometimes another country can make the same goods more cheaply; in other words, it has a comparative advantage. In that case, the two countries will trade.

Austrian Agriculture

About 18 percent of Austria is farmland. While this may not seem like a lot, about 5 percent of all people work in agriculture (compare this to the

THE AUSTRIAN ECONOMY

ABOVE: *In Austria, cattle are grazed on the foothills of the Alps, where the grass is rich enough to produce high-quality milk, cheese, and beef products.*

1 percent of Americans who farm). The country also has about 20,000 organic farms, making it one of the most important countries in Europe for this type of agriculture.

Many agricultural foodstuffs are produced in Austria, including such things as grains, potatoes, and fruit. The country is famous for its high-quality dairy products. It is also a producer of pork, poultry, and beef. Austria has an important wine industry in the east of the country.

EUROPEAN COUNTRIES TODAY: AUSTRIA

Transportation

Austria has an efficient transportation system, with roads, waterways, airlines, and railroads all providing ways to get from one place to another. Vienna in particular has many ways to get around, including streetcars, subways, buses, and commuter trains. This transportation network not only serves to connect Austria's thriving economy, it also connects its people and culture.

Economic Challenge

Like the rest of the world, Austria has faced the economic recession that began in 2008 and continued over the following years. However, because Austria's economy was so strong to start with, it did not experience as serious a problem as other countries. In 2016, Austria's economy was growing by 1.5% and is expected to remain at a similar level throughout 2017–21.

Text-Dependent Questions

1. Name Austria's most important industries.

2. Which countries does Austria export to?

3. What foodstuffs does Austria produce?

Research Project

How is crystal made? What are crystals used for? Swarovski is a leading producer of Austrian crystal. Summarize the company's history.

Words to Understand

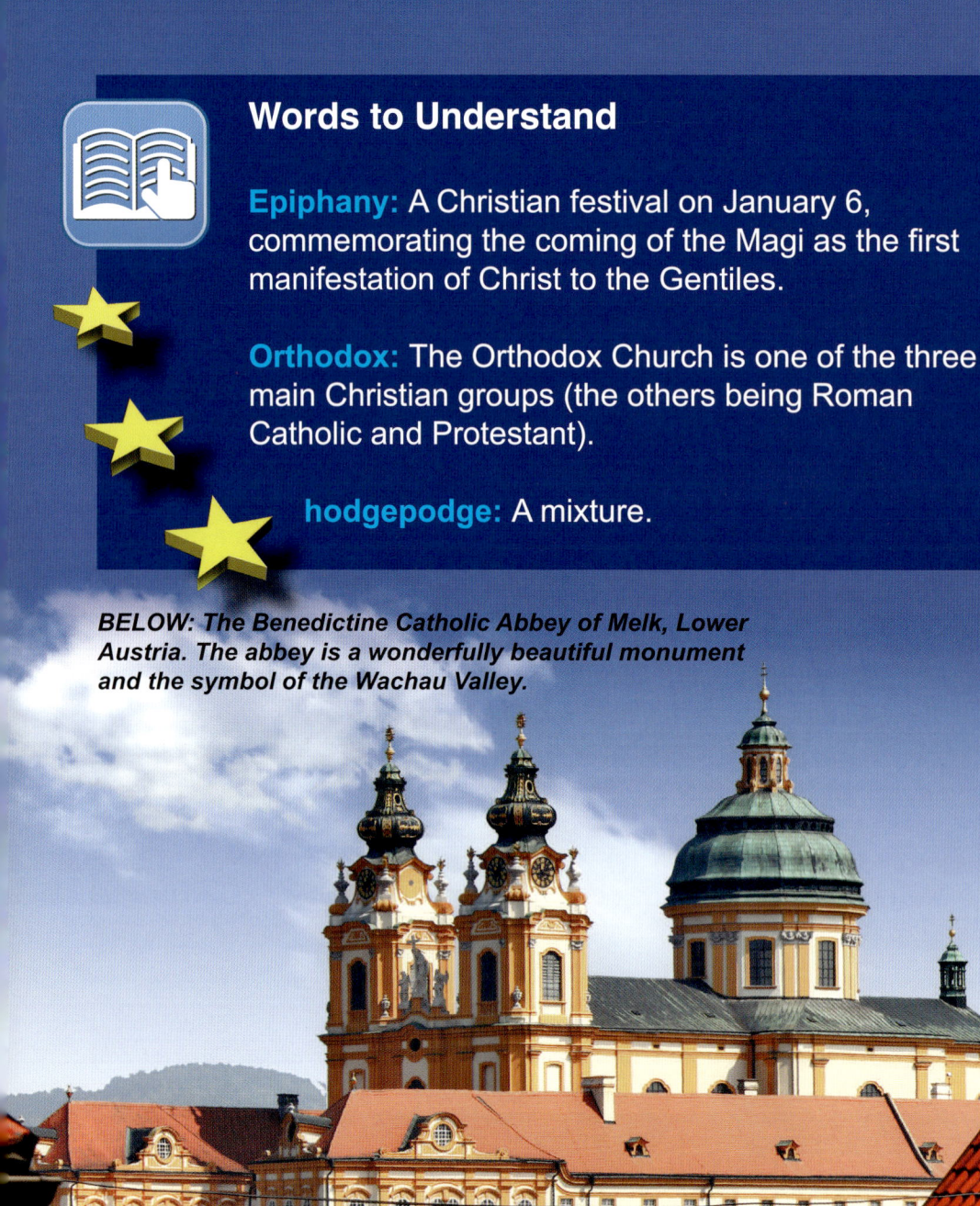

Epiphany: A Christian festival on January 6, commemorating the coming of the Magi as the first manifestation of Christ to the Gentiles.

Orthodox: The Orthodox Church is one of the three main Christian groups (the others being Roman Catholic and Protestant).

hodgepodge: A mixture.

BELOW: *The Benedictine Catholic Abbey of Melk, Lower Austria. The abbey is a wonderfully beautiful monument and the symbol of the Wachau Valley.*

Chapter Four
CITIZENS OF AUSTRIA: PEOPLE, CUSTOMS & CULTURE

Austria is home to over 8.7 million people. Its citizens come from all over Eastern Europe, including Croatia, Slovakia, Hungary, Slovenia, Romania, and the Czech Republic. However, the Ethnic Groups Act of 1976 only recognizes those ethnic groups that have lived in Austria for more than three generations and who are Austrian citizens.

These recognized ethic groups are scattered throughout Austria. In Burgenland are the Croatians and Hungarians. The Slovenians have made their home in the Gail, Rosen, and Jaun valleys in the south, while the Czechs and Slovaks live in Vienna and southern Austria.

No matter what the cultural background of Austrian citizens, they have one thing that ties most of them together: a common language. Ninety-eight percent of the population speaks German.

Religion

In Austria, there is a law which states that everyone over fourteen is allowed to choose their own religion. However, the majority (about 78 percent) is Catholic. This stems from the old Habsburg dynasty, which was a Catholic power. During the Habsburg reign, the government persecuted all non-Catholics. It was not until 1867 that a policy of religious tolerance was put into place, and while everyone is now free to make their own decisions regarding religion, many cling to their old faith.

In 1908, the Austro-Hungarian Empire took control of Bosnia Herzegovina, with its large percentage of Muslims in the population. Because of this, Austria was the first in Europe to officially recognize the Muslim faith. Today, other religious minorities include Protestants, Greek-**Orthodox**, Jews, Mormons, and Buddhists.

CITIZENS OF AUSTRIA: PEOPLE, CUSTOMS & CULTURE

ABOVE: *Roman Catholic Salzburg Cathedral was built in the seventeenth century in the baroque style.*

Catholics are known for their religious education, but in Austria they are not the only providers of religious schools. Many smaller churches and other religious groups also offer education based on their faith. While in the United States these are private schools, and paid for through tuition from the families who attend, in Austria all education—including religious education—is paid for by the state.

Education

The Austrian school system has been developing since Maria Theresa put forth the General School Regulations, a set of guidelines for schools, in 1774. Now all students must attend at least nine years of schooling from the time they are six until age fourteen. If, after that, teens wish to drop out of school, they can attend a polytechnic course that will prepare them for a job.

EUROPEAN COUNTRIES TODAY: AUSTRIA

Educational Video

An American girl studies music at school in Austria.

ABOVE: The Austrian high school, Gymnasium Feldkirch. Austria has a free and public school system, where nine years of education are mandatory.

55

CITIZENS OF AUSTRIA: PEOPLE, CUSTOMS & CULTURE

School starts at the elementary level, which lasts for four years. After that, students attend secondary school. Once this level is completed, there are many choices teens and their families can make. One school is the *allgemein bildende höhere Schule*, which is mostly general education, much like an American high school. Austrian students, however, can either focus on the arts or sciences. Vocational schools are another option, one that provides practical job training to students. After completing either of these types of course, students are issued a certificate, much like a high school diploma, that allows the bearer to apply to a university.

Austrian education is nationally regulated, and all schools are held to the same standards. However, some educators are working toward letting school districts have more freedom in creating their students' curriculum. All schools are free of charge, as are textbooks and transportation to and from school.

Food

Reflecting the diverse population, Austrian food features a great variety of specialties, many of which are known throughout the world. Among these delicacies is *Weiner Schnitzel*, which is fried, breaded veal. Other popular Austrian dishes include *strudels* (pastries made with an apple filling) and *Kaiserschmarrn*, a type of pancake.

In general, Austrians love food with good solid ingredients. They like hearty and flavorsome dishes. Recipes are usually centered around the produce of the region, often focusing on meat, poultry, root vegetables, and dairy. They are famous for their fine desserts, often making use of fruit and chocolate in

ABOVE: *The Weiner Schnitzel is a famous Viennese dish.*

EUROPEAN COUNTRIES TODAY: AUSTRIA

their recipes. Food lovers will adore Austria's fine cheeses, sophisticated white wines, spicy goulash soups (often served in the Alps), while in Vienna, meat dishes are highly recommended. Breakfast consists of bread rolls with jams, cold meats, and cheese, served with coffee and fruit juice.

Gebackene Apfelspaltan (Apple Fritters)

Makes about 24 fritters

Ingredients
1 cup flour
¾ cup milk
1 egg
1 to 2 tablespoons sugar
3 medium apples
Oil for deep frying
Sugar and cinnamon (optional)

Directions
Mix the flour and milk together, and then add egg and sugar. Refrigerate batter for a few hours. When it's cool, blend again to get rid of any lumps that may remain. Peel and core the apples, then cut them into round slices that are about ¼ of an inch thick. (Slice them so that a hole is left in the center where the core used to be. Coat the apply slices in the batter, then fry them in 375°F oil until golden brown on both sides. Remove from the oil and drain on a paper towel. Dust with sugar and cinnamon if desired. Best served warm.

Erdäpfelsalat (Potato Salad)

Ingredients
2 pounds potatoes
1 red onion
2 tablespoons vinegar
4 tablespoons oil
salt and pepper
A small bunch of chopped parsley

Directions
Cook the potatoes while they are still in their skins. Mix the other ingredients in a bowl, and then add the potatoes.

57

CITIZENS OF AUSTRIA: PEOPLE, CUSTOMS & CULTURE

Music & Literature

Austria is very proud of the fact that it is the birthplace of Wolfgang Amadeus Mozart, the prolific composer who wrote hundreds of songs. Many other famous composers called Austria home as well, including Ludwig van Beethoven, Johannes Brahms, Joseph Haydn, Franz Schubert, Johann Strauss Sr., and Johann Strauss Jr. Not all of Austria's musicians lived hundreds of years ago; the country is also home to famous modern groups like Falco and DJ Ötzi.

Austria has produced many famous literary figures as well. One such author, Joseph Roth, became well known for his portrayal of the downfall of the Habsburg Empire. One of his novels, *Savoy Hotel*, tells of life in a hotel and shows it to be a haven for people in trouble who are looking to escape. Another Austrian author is Felix Salten. While the name may not sound familiar, he is the man behind the story *Bambi*, which was later turned into an animated movie by Walt Disney. Other literary figures include Ferdinand Raimond, Ingeborg Bachmann, and Peter Handke.

Arts & Architecture

While many of the Austrian painters are less well known than some of the other artists of similar time periods, the country is still home to much artistic talent. One such artist is

ABOVE: *Mozart (Anonymous).*

ABOVE: *Haydn by Thomas Hardy.*

ABOVE: *Johann Strauss Jr.*

EUROPEAN COUNTRIES TODAY: AUSTRIA

ABOVE: Ludwig van Beethoven by Joseph Karl Stieler.

The Belvedere

The Belvedere is made up of two fine, but distinct, baroque palaces, the unpretentious Lower Belvedere, completed in 1715, where Prince Eugene of Savoy actually lived, and the Upper Belvedere, completed in 1723, a magnificent showpiece used on festive occasions. The architect was Lukas von Hildebrandt, who had fought in Prince Eugene's army and was the greatest Austrian baroque architect after Fischer von Erlach, whom he succeeded (in 1723) as chief architect to the court. Hildebrandt was more Italian than German, having studied in Italy, and the influence of Borromini is evident in the Belvedere, which has been described as "a rare blend of Teutonic solidity and Mediterranean caprice." The interior of the Upper Belvedere is a dazzling assemblage in marble, gold, and inlaid wood, created by a team of architects gathered by Hildebrandt. Like most baroque architects, Hildebrandt rubbed his hands with glee when it came to designing a staircase, which was treated as an individual work of art. In the Upper Belvedere, *putti* play around the almost rococo lamps and vaguely Michelangelesque *atlantes* appear to support the vault and also appear elsewhere. The white marble marvelously lightens the whole structure, which has similarities with an even more attractive staircase (1711) at Pommersfelden in Bavaria, which Hildebrandt placed within a spacious hall with three tiers of galleries.

The Belvedere later passed to the Habsburgs: Marie Antoinette left from here on her way to become queen of France. The composer Bruckner lived in the caretaker's lodgings in his last years, and it was the home of the Archduke Franz Ferdinand, assassinated in Sarajevo in 1914. Today it contains the Austrian Gallery (modern art). Medieval Austrian art can be seen in the orangery of the Lower Belvedere.

CITIZENS OF AUSTRIA: PEOPLE, CUSTOMS & CULTURE

Gustav Klimt (1862–1918)

Klimt was an Austrian symbolist painter and an important member of the Vienna Secession movement. He began his professional life as a successful painter of murals for the public buildings in Vienna and a designer of pageants from the age of the Emperor Franz Joseph.

Klimt and his friends founded a Vienna group to promote modern art, with Klimt as their leader. He was commissioned to produce the murals for the Great Hall of the University of Vienna which at the time sparked controversy. During this time he evolved a personal and highly original style within the Art Nouveau genre that was proliferating throughout Europe.

In the last years of his life, Klimt became a landscape painter, attempting to achieve a closer intimacy with nature through his paintings. Klimts work is not only original, but has decorative qualities very popular today, and appeal among a public which had formerly ignored him because he did not confirm to mainstream art.

Gustav Klimt. Klimt's work dates from the late nineteenth century, and is characterized by intense colors and symbolism, as well as sometimes the use of a gold background. His work was very controversial at the time because of its erotic elements, but he has become very popular with Austrians today. Other Austrian painters include Egon Schiele (1890–1918), Oskar Kokoschka (1886–1980), and Friedensreich Hundertwasser (1928–2000).

Austrian architecture, especially in the city of Vienna, represents a diversity of time periods and styles. The country is a **hodgepodge** of different buildings, from the baroque to the avant-garde styles.

EUROPEAN COUNTRIES TODAY: AUSTRIA

ABOVE: *The Kiss by Gustav Klimt. Oil and gold leaf on canvas, 1907–1908.*

CITIZENS OF AUSTRIA: PEOPLE, CUSTOMS & CULTURE

ABOVE: *The world-famous Christmas market, Vienna.*

EUROPEAN COUNTRIES TODAY: AUSTRIA

Festivals & Events

Austria celebrates many festivals and organizes events throughout the year, some of which can be quite small, while others more significant. Most events center around music; in particular, they celebrate Austria's many composers. The works of famous composers such as Mozart, Beethoven, and Strauss are performed.

Austria also has many religious holidays, like **Epiphany**, Easter, St. Nicolas Day, and Christmas. Austrians celebrate All Souls' Day on November 2 as a time to honor the dead and remember deceased relatives. At this time, it is traditional that gifts and food are left on the graves of the departed. It is also traditional to light candles, and say extra prayers for the deceased.

These festivities are celebrated across Austria, but particularly in the cities, where most Austrians live.

Text-Dependent Questions

1. What are Austria's main ethnic groups?

2. What is Austria's main language?

3. Which dish is made from veal and breadcrumbs?

Research Project

Find out more about Austria's school system. Imagine you are an Austrian student. Which form of education would you choose? Explain why.

Words to Understand

baroque: Refers to an artistic style prevalent especially in the seventeenth century.

château: A stately residence, usually in France or in the French style.

Renaissance: A movement that began in fourteenth-century Italy, reached its height there in the fifteenth century, and then spread to the rest of Europe during the sixteenth and seventeenth centuries.

BELOW: The Vienna skyline showing the grand buildings of the old town. New Vienna is in the background.

Chapter Five
THE FAMOUS CITIES OF AUSTRIA

While there are many small villages and hamlets in Austria, most of the population lives in larger cities. Sixty-eight percent of people live in urban areas, while the rest are spread out throughout the country. Family size in urban areas, as well as the rest of Austria, is relatively small, with most families having one or two children.

These cities are of varied size and population, the largest being Vienna, which is home to about 2 million inhabitants. Other major cities include Graz, Innsbruck, and Salzburg.

Vienna: The Capital of Austria

The most populated city in Austria, Vienna is steeped in history. This city is where the former Habsburg Empire was centered, and many historical buildings from this time can still be seen. Visitors can visit St. Stephen's Cathedral, which continues to reflect the glory and extravagance of the **baroque** era. There is also the Ring, an avenue around the old capitol buildings and palaces that provides a glimpse of historic Austria.

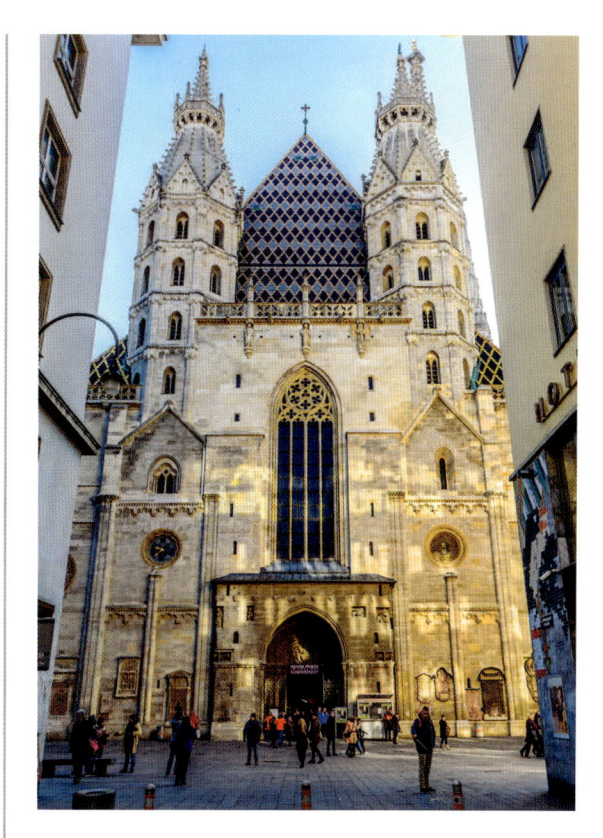

ABOVE: The baroque splendor of St. Stephen's Cathedral, Vienna.

THE FAMOUS CITIES OF AUSTRIA

Educational Video

Vienna and Architecture—Tradition and Modernity. A guided tour of Vienna's rich architectural heritage.

ABOVE: *Donaukanal (Danube Canal), Vienna. On the right is the new UNIQA Tower and left, the historic Urania building, a public educational institute and observatory.*

EUROPEAN COUNTRIES TODAY: AUSTRIA

ABOVE: *The colorful buildings and the Clock Tower in the old town of Graz. It is designated a UNESCO World Cultural Heritage site.*

There are many events that go on in Vienna, including an annual marathon, numerous operas and other musical events, and a ball that is organized every year as an AIDS awareness and fundraising event. At the end of April, a festival is set up in the museum quarter that lasts until September. Here one can see various exhibits, listen to music, and take refreshments that are served in the courtyard next to the museums.

Graz
Situated on the edge of the Alps. The name of the city, Graz, most likely stems from the Slavic *gradec*, meaning "small castle". As time passed, the city grew,

THE FAMOUS CITIES OF AUSTRIA

and now many different types and styles of architecture can be seen there, including the **Renaissance**-style Country House, one of Graz's most well-known buildings. The first Austrian university was built in Graz in 1586, paving the way for the city's tradition of supporting education. Today, the city has at least seven colleges, including medical and art schools.

The city has something for everyone. Graz hosts a jazz festival each summer as well as various film festivals. There are also many sights to see, including the ruins of Gösting Castle. This former **château** was struck by lightning, but it is now one of the most popular spots to visit in the city.

ABOVE: *Eggenberg Palace is the most important and biggest baroque palace in Styria and has been a UNESCO World Heritage Site since 2010.*

EUROPEAN COUNTRIES TODAY: AUSTRIA

Innsbruck

The name of this city comes from an old bridge to the town inn that runs over a stream, formerly in the center of the town. The city's coat of arms portrays this bridge, leading to its name.

Innsbruck is a very athletic city; almost any physical activity that one can imagine goes on here—rock climbing, sky diving, mountain biking, and skateboarding, to name a few. Innsbruck, like the rest of Austria, also places great emphasis on music and the arts and is home to the National Theater.

ABOVE: *The historical center of Innsbruck.*

THE FAMOUS CITIES OF AUSTRIA

2012 Winter Youth Olympic Games

Officially known as the Winter Youth Olympic Games, the Games are an international multisport event for youths. The 2012 games took place in Innsbruck on 1 January 13–22 2012. These games were the inaugural Winter Youth Olympics. It was a major sports and cultural festival conducted in the tradition of the Olympic Games. Approximately 1100 athletes from 70 countries competed. The decision to host the Games in Innsbruck was announced on December 12, 2008 after a vote by 105 International Olympic Committee members. In addition to the Youth Olympic Games, Innsbruck has now hosted three winter Olympic events, the other two being the 1964 Winter Olympics and the 1976 Winter Olympics.

ABOVE: *Marcel Godbout (USA) and Eduard Nasybullin (Russia) fight for the puck in the ice hockey tournament at the 2012 Winter Youth Olympic Games.*

EUROPEAN COUNTRIES TODAY: AUSTRIA

THE FAMOUS CITIES OF AUSTRIA

ABOVE: *The city of Salzburg with the river Salzach flowing through it. The city and river gained their names from the salt that has been mined in the region for centuries.*

Salzburg

Salzburg is the birthplace of the musician Mozart. Because of this, many festivals celebrating his music take place throughout the year. The city is very proud of its most famous resident, and visitors can still see the house where this child prodigy was born.

As well as being home to one of the most well-known composers of all time, Salzburg is also where the musical *The Sound of Music* takes place. What some don't know is that the von Trapp family really existed and lived in Salzburg in the 1930s. Mr von Trapp hired a former nun as a nanny for his children, who then persuaded the family to turn their love of singing together

EUROPEAN COUNTRIES TODAY: AUSTRIA

Hohensalzburg Castle

Hohensalzburg Castle, literally meaning "High Salzburg Fortress," sits atop the Festungsberg, a rocky outcrop in Salzburg. Erected at the command of the prince-archbishops of Salzburg, it is one of the largest medieval castles in Europe.

Construction of the fortress began in 1077 under Archbishop Gebhard von Helfenstein. The castle was later expanded to the size it is today by Prince-Archbishop Leonhard von Keutschach during his reign from 1495 until 1519.

The castle was refurbished from the late nineteenth century onwards, and has become became a major tourist attraction. It stands today as one of the best- preserved castles in Europe.

During the early twentieth century it was used as a prison, holding Italian prisoners of war during World War I, and then Nazi supporters in the 1930s.

Schloss Leopoldskron & The Sound of Music

Schloss Leopoldskron is a rococo palace and a national historic monument in Leopoldskron-Moos, a district of Salzburg. The palace, and its surrounding large park, is located on lake Leopoldskroner Weiher. It was used as a location in *The Sound of Music* film, starring Julie Andrews and Christopher Plummer. The film was based on a musical by Richard Rodgers and Oscar Hammerstein II from a book by Howard Lindsay and Russel Crouse. It is based on the memoir of Maria von Trapp, *The*

Story of the Trapp Family Singers. Set in Austria on the eve of the Anschluss in 1938, the musical tells the story of Maria, who takes a job as governess to a large family while she decides whether to become a nun. She falls in love with the children, and eventually with their widowed father, Captain von Trapp. He is ordered to accept a commission in the German navy, but he opposes the Nazis. He and Maria decide on a plan to flee Austria with the children. Many songs from the musical have become standards, such as "Edelweiss," "My Favorite Things," "Climb Ev'ry Mountain," "Do-Re-Mi," and the title song "The Sound of Music."

THE FAMOUS CITIES OF AUSTRIA

into a moneymaking venture in which they were paid for performing. Once Hitler came to power, the family fled to America, leaving everything they owned behind them. Eventually, they made their fortune in the United States, where they became famous and toured until 1956.

How Salzburg Got Its Name

The magnificent city of Salzburg is famous for its salt mines. *Salz* is the German word for salt. The city of Salzburg (and the surrounding region of Salzkammergut) was named after its abundant salt deposits. The oldest salt mine in the world is at Hallein, near Salzburg. Salt mining in the region dates back to the era of the Celts, when salt was first mined to preserve food and give it flavor. Throughout the centuries, rulers of Salzburg traded in salt, making lucrative profits, with opulent, residences built with the proceeds. The salt mine at Hallein is no longer used, but Austria's salt supplies still come from the surrounding mountains.

These cities form Austria's backbone. All three are known for their fascinating architecture dating back to ancient times. Today they are important tourist attractions known for their modern architecture, culture, cuisine, and shopping.

ABOVE: *Hallstatt is considered to be the most beautiful village in Europe. It is close to Hallein Salt Mine and situated in the Salzkammergut region.*

EUROPEAN COUNTRIES TODAY: AUSTRIA

ABOVE: A large block of orange salt in a mine in near Salzburg.

Text-Dependent Questions

1. What is the name of Vienna's cathedral?

2. What city did Mozart come from?

3. What city established the first Austrian University?

Research Project

Find out more about the *Anschluss* and how it affected Austria.

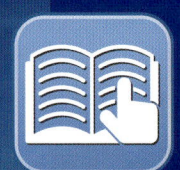

Words to Understand

discrimination: The treatment of, or making a distinction in favor of or against, a person based on the group, class, or category to which that person or thing belongs rather than on individual merit.

renewable: Capable of being replaced by natural ecological cycles or sound management practices.

stability: The strength to stand or endure.

BELOW: Skier taking in the view of the magnificent Austrian Alps.

Chapter Six
A BRIGHT FUTURE FOR AUSTRIA

Austria has come a long way. Less than sixty years ago, the country became independent after a nine-year occupation following World War II. Since then, Austria has certainly secured her place in the world. Austrians are enthusiastic about integrating EU policies, but the country has also led the way toward healthier trends for society, the environment, and the economy.

The European Union's Influence

Austria has a long history, but it has only been part of the EU for a mere fraction of that time. The effects of joining the European Union, however, have been immense. Most of its recent economic success can be attributed to its membership of the EU. This is due to more than just increased trade.

The Common Agricultural Policy was originally created under the Treaties of Rome in 1957. It has changed drastically since that time, but over the years it has helped regulate the agricultural industry across all nations involved. Austria's agricultural products include grains, potatoes, dairy, meat, vegetables, fruit, and wine. Although agriculture

ABOVE: *EU and Austrian flags.*

A BRIGHT FUTURE FOR AUSTRIA

ABOVE: *Austria has embraced the euro which unlike other countries such as Sweden and the UK, have kept their own currency.*

is not even close to being the greatest source of Austria's income, this particular policy has helped protect the jobs of many farmers in the nation.

Despite the benefits, joining the EU has brought about changes that some Austrians find difficult to accept. As is the case with other issues as well, being a member of the EU requires that Austria's government give up some of its power in order to follow the policies set forth by the union. Some people, used to being completely independent, dislike handing over their power to an international organization. This tension has become particularly noticeable in the past few years during large shifts in political power.

Social & Cultural Implications

Austria is a successful country and therefore can allocate a healthy budget for arts and culture. However, recent austerity measures have meant some financial cuts to funding in this area.

EUROPEAN COUNTRIES TODAY: AUSTRIA

Austria's Economy

Austria is one of the richest countries in the world in terms of GDP (gross domestic product) per capita, it has a well-developed social market economy and a high standard of living. Until the 1980s, many of Austria's largest industry firms were nationalized; in recent years, however, privatization has reduced state holdings to a level comparable to other European economies. Labor movements are particularly strong in Austria and have a great deal of influence over labor politics. Next to its highly developed industry, international tourism is the most important part of the national economy.

Trade with other EU countries accounts for about two-thirds of Austrian imports and exports. Expanding trade and investment in the emerging markets of Central and Eastern Europe is a major element of Austrian economic activity, and trade with these countries accounts for a substantial volume of Austrian imports and exports. Austrian firms have sizable investments in these countries, and continue to move labor-intensive, low-tech production. Although the big investment boom has waned, Austria still has the potential to attract EU firms seeking convenient access to these developing markets.

ABOVE: *Vienna's financial district with the river Danube in the foreground.*

83

A BRIGHT FUTURE FOR AUSTRIA

The Austrian government supports contemporary art, funds improvements to working conditions in cultural fields, and arts in schools. Also, general funding is granted to aid theaters, museums, libraries, and the film industry. New policies have been put into place to protect historical buildings, monuments, and other forms of cultural heritage as well.

If Austria's current trend of economic growth continues, funding for these cultural programs will likely to continue to increase. This will not only preserve Austria's cultural heritage, but will also encourage the creation of new works of art and culture.

ABOVE: Buildings in Austria's historic cities and towns such as Melk are protected, and have been given funding to aid renovations.

EUROPEAN COUNTRIES TODAY: AUSTRIA

ABOVE: Artstetten Castle is a château near the Wachau Valley, Lower Austria. An image of it has featured on a ten-euro collectors' coin.

A BRIGHT FUTURE FOR AUSTRIA

Austria also supports legislation that protects the rights of all human beings. **Discrimination** and prejudice against Roma, Turks, and other groups continue to be a reality, but the government is working hard to promote tolerance and equal rights for all human beings within Austria's borders.

Education is one way to do this. Public higher education in Austria is relatively cheap. A small tuition fee is charged on a per-semester basis and the amount depends on whether you are an EU student or have come to study in Austria from a country outside Europe. The cost is a tiny fraction of the cost of college in the United States.

A low-cost education means a brighter future and further advances for the country. Austria's policies give a person from any background the chance to be just as successful as anyone else. And unlike countries such as the United

ABOVE: Hydro power is Austria's main source of electricity. This plant is on the Traun River in Marchtrenk.

EUROPEAN COUNTRIES TODAY: AUSTRIA

ABOVE: *Power plant using renewable solar energy in the Alps at Hohen Tauren.*

States, attending university in Austria will not put you in debt for years to come! However, low cost and easy accessibility to university-level education has a number of consequences. The dramatic expansion in the number of students can lead to overcrowding at many institutions. Some critics maintain that the increasing number of students diminishes the overall quality of university-level education despite increases in federal investment. Generally speaking, a university degree provides students with improved social status and better income opportunities, although "academic unemployment" can often be a problem.

Energy Conservation

Austria is one of only a few countries that obtain more than fifty percent of their energy from **renewable** energy sources. Over half the electricity in Austria is

A BRIGHT FUTURE FOR AUSTRIA

ABOVE: *Wind energy plant near Parndorf.*

generated from hydroelectric power. Together with wind, biomass, geothermal, and solar power, renewable energy sources make up almost sixty percent of all electrical energy consumed in Austria. Due to a law passed several decades ago, the use of nuclear power is forbidden in the country.

The policies of the European Union require member countries to work toward certain standards. Austria is leading the way in development for cleaner energy.

Highlights

In 2012, Austria hosted the first Youth Winter Olympics, for athletes between the ages of fourteen and eighteen. The games held in Innsbruck, a city in the western part of Austria. In the past, Previously, Innsbruck hosted the Winter Olympic Games in 1964 and 1976. The city has also hosted the 1984 and 1988

EUROPEAN COUNTRIES TODAY: AUSTRIA

Paralympics. Austria was chosen to host the Youth Winter Olympics partly because the organizers knew the country had the expertise to host an Olympic event. In addition, Austria's financial **stability** meant they would make a successful Olympic host.

The 2017 Special Olympics World Winter Games were held in Graz and Schladming in Styria, Austria. The event is the biggest international sport movement for people with intellectual disabilities. The Special Olympics is a movement whose aim is to establish a new world of inclusion and community, where each individual is accepted and included, irrespective of their abilities or disabilities.

As a member of the European Union, Austria is thriving and stable. The people of Austria face many challenges—but they look toward a bright tomorrow, ready to face whatever lies ahead.

Text-Dependent Questions

1. Why does Austria fund its arts and culture?

2. Which method of power generation is forbidden in Austria?

3. What are the Special Olympics World Winter Games?

Research Project

How many sources of renewable energy does Austria use? Describe how each kind of renewable energy is generated.

CHRONOLOGY

80,000–10,000 BCE	Austria is settled.
0	The Romans control the land that is now Austria.
700 CE	Charlemagne takes over the territory.
900s	Magyars from Hungary attack and conquer Austria.
955	Otto the Great vanquishes the Magyars.
1500s	The Ottoman Empire invades.
1600s	The Ottomans are defeated.
1618	The Protestants rebel against the Catholic Habsburg emperor, leading to the Thirty Years' War.
1648	The Peace of Westphalia ends the war, making Austria a Roman Catholic nation.
1701–1714	Austria and France fight the War of Spanish Succession (Austria wins Belgium and Spain's Italian lands).
1700s–1815	The Napoleonic Wars.
1815	Napoleon is defeated.
1859	Austria declares war on Sardinia and is defeated by Italy and France.
1867	The Austro-Hungarian Empire comes into being.
1914	Archduke Franz Ferdinand is assassinated and World War I starts.
1918	World War I ends.
1918	The last Habsburg emperor is overthrown and the Austrian Republic is formed.
1938	Hitler seizes control of Austria.
1939	World War II starts.
1945	The Allies defeat Germany.
1945	Austrian territory is divided between the United States, Britain, France, and the Soviet Union.
1954	The occupation of Austria ends.
1995	Austria joins the EU.
2016	Alexander Van der Bellen defeats Norbert Hofer in the re run of the presidential election.
2017	300 years since the birth of Maria Theresa.

FURTHER READING & INTERNET RESOURCES

Further Reading

Di Duca, Mark. Christiani, Kerry. Le Nevez, Catherine. Wheeler, Donna. *Lonely Planet Austria (Travel Guide)*. London: Lonely Planet Publications, 2017.

Kumlanlecka, Janina. Ewa, Dan. Dudek, Marianna. Gruda, Konrad. Omilanowska, Malgorzata. Pernal, Marek. Sito, Jakup. Wojcikowska-Sudnik, Barbara. Taborski, Roman. Umer, Zuzanna. *DK Eyewitness Travel Guide: Austria*. London: DK, 2016.

McCormick, John. *Understanding the European Union: A Concise Introduction.* London: Palgrave Macmillan, 2017.

Mason, David S. *A Concise History of Modern Europe: Liberty, Equality, Solidarity.* London: Rowman & Littlefield, 2015.

Internet Resources

Austria Travel Information and Travel Guide
www.lonelyplanet.com/austria

Austrian National Tourism Office
www.austriatourism.com

Austria: Country Profile
http://www.bbc.co.uk/news/world-europe-17405422

Austria: CIA World Factbook
https://www.cia.gov/library/publications/the-world-factbook/geos/au.html

The Official Website of the European Union
europa.eu/index_en.htm

Publisher's note:
The websites listed on this page were active at the time of publication. The publisher is not responsible for websites that have changed their addresses or discontinued operation since the date of publication. The publisher will review and update the website list upon each reprint.

INDEX

A
Aachen, Hans von, 25
Age of population, 9
Agriculture, 49–50, 81–82
Allgemein bildende höhere Schule, 56
All Souls' Day, 65
Alpine region, 11–12
Alps, 13, 50, 69, 79, 87
Amerling, Friedrich von, 29
Andrews, Julie, 76
Anschluss, 76–77
Anti-Semitism, 32, 34
Archduke Ferdinand II (Terzi), 28
Architecture, 62
Area, 7, 11
Art, 58–63å
Art Nouveau, 62
Artstetten Castle, 85
Assassination, 32, 35, 60
Atlantes, 60
Attersee, 12
Austerity measures, 82
Austrian
    Gallery, 60
        Mineral Oil Administration, 43
        Parliament Building, 36, 37
Austrians, 9
Austro-Hungarian Empire, 8, 32, 53
    dissolution of, 32, 34
Avalanches, 7

B
Babenbergs, 24
Bachmann, Ingeborg, 58
Balkan frog, 18
Bambi (Salten), 58
Baroque era, 67
Bavaria, 60
Beethoven, Ludwig van, 58, 59
Belgium, 41
Bellen, Alexander Van der, 39
Belvedere, 60–61
Benedictine Catholic Abbey of Melk, 52
Birds, 17
Birth rate, 9
"Blue Danube" (Strauss), 12
Boar, wild, 17
Bohemia, 24
Bonaparte, Napoleon, 31
Borders, 7, 34
Borromini, 60
Bosnia Herzegovina, 53
Brahms, Johannes, 58
Bruckner, 60
Brussels, 40
Buddhism, 53
Business
    nationalization of, 83
    privatization, 43, 83
    smaller, 45–46

C
Campanula (bellflower), 15
Capital, 67
Carinthia, 19
Castles, 18
Cattle, 9, 50
Celtic tribes, 23
Central Powers, 32
Chamois, 14
Charlemagne, 23, 24
Charlemagne (Dürer), 23
Château, 70
Chemical manufacturing, 46
China, 49
Christian Social Party, 32
Christmas, 65
Cities, 67–79
Climate, 7
"Climb Ev'ry Mountain," 77
Clock Tower, 69
Common Agricultural Policy, 81
Computers, 46
Confederation of the Rhine, 31
Constantinople, 28
Counter Revolution, 28
Country House, 70
Craft-making, 45

Crimean War, 32
Croatian language, 9
Croatians, 53
Crouse, Russel, 76
Crystal, 45
Czech Republic, 7, 11, 48, 49
Czechs, 53

D
Dairy products, 50
Danube
    basin, 12
    canal, 68
    River, 12, 22, 23, 83
    warty newt, 18
David, Jacques Louis, 31
Death rate, 9
Discrimination, 86
DJ Ötzi, 58
Dolfus, Chancellor Engelbert, 34–35
Donau-Auen National Park, 18
Donau City, 38
Donaukanal (Danube Canal), 68
"Do-Re-Mi," 77
Dürer, Albrecht, 23

E
Earthquakes, 7
Easter, 65
Economy, 43–51, 83
    growth, 84
Edelweiss, 14
"Edelweiss," 77
Education, 54–56, 86
    levels, 56
Eggenberg Palace, 70
Election, first, 32
Elevation extremes, 7
Emperor Rudolf II (von Aachen), 25
Empire of Austria, 31
Energy
    conservation, 87–88
    renewable, 87
Epiphany, 65

92

INDEX

Erdäpfelsalat (potato salad), 57
Erlach
    Fisher von, 60
    Johann Fischer von, 26–27
    Josef Emanuel von, 27
Ethnic groups, 9
Ethnic Groups Act of 1976, 53
Eugene of Savoy, Prince, 28, 60
Eurasian
    brown bear, 17
    lynx, 17
Euro, 82
European
    Coal and Steel Community, 41
    Council, 40
    Free Trade Association, 36
European Union (EU), 36, 89
    flag, 81
    formation of, 40–41
    influence, 81–82
    members, 40, 41
    Parliament Building, 40
Exports, 48–49, 83

F
Falco, 58
February Edict, 32
Federal
    Assembly, 36
    Council, 36
Ferdinand II, Archduke, 28
Fertility rate, 9
Festivals, 65
Festungsberg, 75
Flag, 8, 81
Föhn, 11
Food, 48, 56–57
Forests, 13
France, 35, 40, 41, 48, 49
Francis (Franz) II, Holy Roman Emperor (von Amerling), 30
Franz
    Ferdinand, Archduke, 32, 33, 60
    II, Emperor, 29, 30, 31

Joseph I, Emperor, 32, 62
Freedom, 31
Freedom Party, 36, 39
French Revolution, 29, 31
Friedrich II, King, 29

G
Gail valley, 53
Gebackene Apfelspaltan (apple fritters), 57
General School Regulations, 54
Geography, 7
German
    Empire, 32
    language, 9
Germans, 9
Germany, 11, 34, 40, 41, 48, 49
Gesäuse National Park, 20–21
Godbout, Marcel, 72–73
Golden eagle, 16
Gösting Castle, 70
Government
    funding, 84
    modern, 36, 39
Graz, 69–70, 89
Great
    Britain, 35
    Hall of the University of Vienna, 62
Greek-Orthodox, 53
Gross domestic product (GDP), 45, 49, 83
Grossglockner, 7, 11–12
Grouse, 17
Gymnasium Feldkirch, 55

H
Habsburg, Rudolf von, 24
Habsburgs, 24, 26, 28, 53, 58, 60, 67
Hallein, 78
Hallstatt, 78
Hammerstein, Oscar, II, 76
Handke, Peter, 58
Hardegg Castle, 19
Haydn, Joseph, 58

Haydn (Hardy), 58
Helfenstein, Archbishop Gebhard von, 75
Hildebrandt, Lukas von, 60
History, 23–36
Hitler, Adolf, 35
Hohensalzburg Castle, 75
Hohen Tauren, 87
Hohe Tauern National Park, 19
Holland, 24
Holy Roman Empire. *See* Roman Empire
Hundertwasser, Friedensreiche, 62
Hungarian language, 9
Hungarians, 53
Hungary, 7, 11, 24
Hydroelectricity, 44, 46, 86, 88

I
Ibex, 17
Imports, 48–49, 83
    partners, 49
Industries, 45–46, 49
Infant mortality rate, 9
Inflation, 34
Innsbruck, 71, 72, 88
International Olympic Committee, 72
Iron, 46
Islam, 9, 53
Italy, 7, 11, 41, 48, 49

J
Jaun valley, 53
Johann Strauss, Jr., 58
Josef, Franz, Emperor, 12
Joseph II, 29
Judaism, 53. *See also* Anti-Semitism

K
Kaiserschmarrn, 56
Kalkalpen National Park, 19–20
Kaprun, 44
Karl VI, Emperor, 29

93

INDEX

Keutschach, Prince-Archbishop Leonhard von, 75
Kiss, The (Klimt), 63
Klimt, Gustav, 62, 63
Kokoschka, Oskar, 62
Kurz, Sebastian, 39

L
Labor movements, 83
Lake
    Langbathsee, 12
    Neusiedl, 12, 13, 17
Landslides, 7
Languages, 9
League of Nations, 34
Leopold
    Emperor, 26
    V, Duke, 8
Leopoldskron-Moos, 76
Liechtenstein, 7, 11
Life expectancy, 9
Lindsay, Howard, 76
Literacy rate, 9
Literature, 58
Location, 7
Lombardy, 32
Ludwig van Beethoven (Stieler), 59
Lumber, 46
Luxembourg, 41
Lynx, 17

M
Maastricht Treaty, 41
Machinery, 46
Map, 6
Marchtenk, 86
Maria Theresa, Empress, 27, 29, 54
Maria Theresa (Meytens), 29
Marie Antoinette, 29, 60
Maximilian, Emperor, 26
Melk, 84
Merger Treaty, 41
Meytens, Martin van, 29
Migration rate, 9

Militias, 34
Mooser Dam, 44
Mormonism, 53
Mountains, 8, 11–12
Mozart, 58
Mozart, Wolfgang Amadeus, 58, 74
    home of, 46
Mummy, 23
Music, 58
Mussolini, 34
"My Favorite Things," 77

N
Napoleon. *See* Bonaparte, Napoleon
Napoleon Bonaparte (David), 31
Naschmarkt, 8
Nasybullin, Eduard, 72–73
Nationalist Socialist Party, 34
National Theater, 71
Natural gas, 46
Netherlands, 41
Neusiedler, 7
    See-Seewinkel National Park, 18
Nockberge
    Biosphere Reserve, 21
    Mountains, 21

O
Occupation
    Allied, 8, 35
    German, 8, 35
October Diploma, 32
Oil, 43, 46
Orthodox Christian, 9
Ottokar, King, 24
Ottomans, 28
Otto the Great, 24

P
Pacassi, Nikolaus, 27
Paleolithic Age, 23
Paralympics, 89
Parks, national, 14, 18–21

Parliament, 36
Parndorf, 88
Peace of Westphalia, 28
People, 9
People's Party, 36
Pinzgauer, 9
Pinzgau region, 9
Plants, Alpine, 14
Plummer, Christopher, 76
Political parties, 32, 36
Pommersfelden, 60
Poor, 45
Population, 9
    age, 9
    growth rate, 9
Precipitation, 11–12
Protestant, 9
    Revolution, 28
Protestantism, 28–29, 53
Prussia, 29
Putti, 60

R
Raimond, Ferdinand, 58
Recession, economic, 51
Reconstruction, 35–36
Religion, 9, 53–54
    choice, freedom of, 53
Renaissance style, 70
Reparation, 35
Ring, 67
Riots, 34
Rodgers, Richard, 76
Roman Catholic church, 28
Roman Catholicism, 9, 54
Roman Empire, 23–24, 28, 29, 31
Rosen valley, 53
Roth, Joseph, 58
Rudolf II, Emperor, 25

S
Saint Helen, 31
Salten, Felix, 58
Salt mines, 78, 79
Salzach river, 74

INDEX

Salzburg, 19, 46, 74–78
    Cathedral, 54
    name origin, 78
Sarajevo, 60
Savoy Hotel (Roth), 58
Schiele, Egon, 62
Schladming, 89
Schloss Leopoldskron, 76–77
Schönbrunn Palace, 26–27
Schönbühel Castle, 22
Schubert, Franz, 58
Schuschnigg, Kurt von, 35
Schwechat, 43
Secularization of monasteries, 29
Serbian language, 9
Serfdom, abolishment, 29
Seven Years' War, 29
Siege of Acre, 8
Silesia, 29
Silesian War, 29
Size, 11
Skiing, 79
Slovakia, 7, 11
Slovaks, 53
Slovene language, 9
Slovenia, 7, 11
Slovenians, 53
Social Democratic Party, 32, 36
Socialism, 34–35
Social security system, 45
Solar energy, 87
Sound of Music, The, 74, 76–77, 78
"Sound of Music, The," 77
Southeast region, 11
Spain, 24
Special Olympics World Winter Games, 89
Sports, 47
St.
    Nicolas Day, 65
    Stephen's Cathedral, 67
Starvation, 34
Steel, 46
Stieler, Joseph Karl, 59
Story of the Trapp Family

Singers, The (von Trapp), 76–77
Strauss
    Johann, 12
    Johann, Jr., 58
    Johann, Sr., 58
Strudels, 56
Styria, 70, 89
Swarovski, 45
Switzerland, 7, 11, 48, 49

T
Terrain, 7
Terzi, Francesco, 28
Thaya, 18
Thayatal National Park, 18
Third Crusade, 8
Thirty Years' War, 28
Tirol, 19
Toleration policy, 28
Tourism, 45, 46, 83
Trade, 36
Transportation, 51
Trapp
    Captain von, 77
    family von, 74
    Maria von, 76–77
Traun River, 86
Traunsee, 12
Treaties of Rome, 41, 81
Treaty of
    Paris, 41
    Saint-Germain, 34
Triple Alliance, 32
Turkey, 32
Turkish language, 9

U
Umlaufberg, 18
UNIQA Tower, 68
United
    Nations, 35
    States, 32, 35, 48, 49, 86–87
University, 87
Urania building, 68
USSR, 35

V
Valleys, 11
Vegetation, 13–14, 15
Versailles, 27
Vienna, 8, 26–27, 34, 36, 37, 38, 53, 62, 65, 67–69, 83
    basin, 12
    Christmas market, 64
Vienna Secession movement, 62
Vocational schools, 56
Voting age, 39

W
Wachau, 22
    Valley, 52, 85
Waldheim, Kurt, 36
War of Spanish Succession, 28
Water, bodies of, 12
Waterloo, 31
Wattens, 45
Weiner Schnitzel, 56
West Germany, 40, 41
White Lake, 20
Wildlife, 14, 16, 17
    endangered, 17
Wind, 11
    energy, 88
Winemaking industry, 42, 50
Winter
    Olympic Games, 88
    Youth Olympic Games 2012, 72–73, 88, 89
World War
    I, 32, 34
    II, 8, 36, 43

Y
Yugoslavs, 9

Picture Credits

All images in this book are in the public domain or have been supplied under license by © Shutterstock.com. The publisher credits the following images as follows:
Page 8: Radiokafka, page 38: Maciej Bledowski, page 40: Roman Yanushevsky, page 46: Damira, page 64: Posztos, page 67: Sumit.kumar99, page 72: Herbert Kratky, page 84 Karara.

To the best knowledge of the publisher, all images not specifically credited are in the public domain. If any image has been inadvertently uncredited, please notify the publisher, so that credit can be given in future printings.

Video Credits

Page 12 Geography Now!: http://x-qr.net/1Es8
page 24 Smithsonian Channel: http://x-qr.net/1F2y
page 46 ADVANTAGE AUSTRIA: http://x-qr.net/1EEe
page 55 GoGreenheartTravel: http://x-qr.net/1EfD
page 68 Austria TVC Collection: http://x-qr.net/1Fp8

Author

Dominic J. Ainsley is a freelance writer on history, geography, and the arts and the author of many books on travel. His passion for traveling dates from when he visited Europe at the age of ten with his parents. Today, Dominic travels the world for work and pleasure, documenting his experiences and encounters as he goes. He lives in the south of England in the United Kingdom with his wife and two children.